Legendary
TEAM
Leadership

By W.W. Peche
With Pat Gray Thomas

Cataloging-in-Publication Data

Peche, Wendy W.
    Legendary team leadership / Wendy W. Peche
    p. cm.
    Includes bibliographical references and index.
    ISBN 0-9630727-1-4

    1. Leadership. 2. Management. I. Title
HD57.7.P43 1994   658.4
                QBI94-1793

Printed in the U.S.A.

Dedicated to my home team—
Leroy and Lauren

Acknowledgments

Many people have played a part in the creation of this book. To our families who gave encouragement and insight while awaiting the finish of this LEGENDARY book, thank you. There would not be a book without your counsel and your unflagging support.

To friends, many who are not cited here due to the surprising end of empty pages, and coworkers, we are forever grateful:

To Shirley Hicks, who from the start of Teamwork By Design, to transcribing the LEGENDARY interviews and compiling its index, has been a researcher and executive assistant without equal.

To Peggy Allen Weber, our computer expert, for patience and persistence and producing copy after copy until we got it right.

To Thomas L. Nolan, Jr., our publisher, for his knowledge and experience, and his ability to listen.

To Ronald L. Heilmann, for his crucial role in helping to define the eight fundamental elements and refocus the LEGENDARY vision.

To Howard Schlei, whose perception and creative skills brought our cover to life.

To Pat Gahl, for lending the business and marketing acumen that every publication needs for success.

To Timothy J. Richman, who listened endlessly and helped guide LEGENDARY's development.

To Valerie Adams for the wit and wisdom that helps to sharpen ideas, words and writers.

To Richard Skews, who shared his vacation with our manuscript and gave LEGENDARY clearance for closing.

Back to the beginning, a most important thank you to the coaches for their time and cooperation over these many months, and for their inspiration that led to and underlies LEGENDARY TEAM LEADERSHIP.

A finale of thunderous applause is given to those who gave their editorial and/or artistic skills at countless points in this project: Mary Jabsen, Julia Liesse, Joan Lloyd, Michael Ryan,

Geoffrey Shives. And to all the public record holders that answered every inquiry within minutes: the Harold Washington Library in Chicago, the NBA, the NCAA, the International Women's Sports Foundation, USA Basketball, and the many universities represented herein, you are golden.

Table of Contents

Prologue

Teamwork: In the year 2000, it is estimated that 90% of all United States companies will organize their work force in teams. No wonder effective team building is identified by business leaders as one of the top seven most desired skills wanted in the 1990s.

Although most of us in the U.S. business community are keenly aware of Japanese teamwork success stories, we frequently forget the legendary team leadership practiced for decades not far from our own back yards: in our schools, in old sand lots, in new parks and in high school and college stadiums. For most of us the introduction to team leadership takes place close to home, and there too is where our love affair with sports usually begins. But, as the years pass, our knowledge and perception of team leadership is most often tied to wins and losses rather than the quality of skill and/or style.

Athletics entered my life just a few years after my legs would carry me beyond the local park. The love of sports started for me on a golf course. And while the challenge of and my love for the game continued, the complexity and excitement of team sports began to capture my attention in junior high school. From then until soon after college, when my interest in team sports catapulted into a passion for teamwork, I was both participant and observer of teamwork and team leadership. For most of my life I have played on and worked in teams; I've observed and studied teams; I have led teams and followed teams, both winners and losers, and in my professional life I have been training teams for close to 15 years. The teamwork process still fascinates me.

In retrospect, that fascination began to shape this book in 1987, when I started a management consulting and training company, Teamwork By Design, in Milwaukee. This included a quarterly newsletter that featured an interview with a prominent business or sports leader talking about team leadership. In May, 1991, I interviewed Dick Bennett, the University of Wisconsin-Green Bay, basketball coach. What I learned about team leadership from that experience was the catalyst for this book. I realized that Dick Bennett and other coaches like him could synthesize their knowledge of and share their passion for team leadership on a level I had never imagined.

Successful team leaders in the sports world have been using teamwork concepts longer than many of us can recall. However, while coaches deal with many of the issues that confront work force leaders, i.e.:

- balancing individual vs team needs,
- personality conflicts,
- maximizing varying skill levels,
- different motivational needs,
- problem solving,
- limited time and resources,
- high expectations inside & outside the team,

the sports world is not a mirror image of the business world. We are quick to see that most business/industry leaders do not deal with multiple **stars**, nor do they suffer national observation and analysis by countless critics, across the country or around the world, week after week, year after year!

Four years ago when my first thoughts about writing a story or a book on teamwork began to crystalize, I knew that the old idea promoting independence and individuality as the road to success was losing followers; internal competition was no longer productive; short-term goals were stifling growth, and the past, while retaining its relevance, was certainly not always reliable. In addition, and regardless of the business or the level of the players, there is awareness that we cannot compete externally unless we cooperate internally.

All of these changes create an environment that makes teamwork the most attractive and historically successful approach to faltering businesses. However, although a more educated work force is able and eager to participate in setting, planning and achieving organization goals, this management process—which brings directors and players onto the same floor—must have a leader. For ultimately, team building success is dependent on the quality of its leadership. Also, it is imperative that all participants be astute listeners, ready to understand and utilize the ideas from the combined voices that produce a more knowledgeable, a stronger and a more effective successful group:

TOGETHER
EVERYONE
ACCOMPLISHES
MORE

TEAM

In my years of experience, internal cooperation—or more pointedly its absence—underlies almost every question or problem that prompts an executive to call for help in restructuring company policy and/or procedures. The potential client always asks me: "How do we work better together? How do we improve our working relationships? How do we develop teamwork?" Before any answer is offered, I need to know: "Are the top executives involved?"

My response to a client begins with a simple explanation for my question:

TEAM DEVELOPMENT
MUST BEGIN AT THE TOP

I repeat, because it is extremely important: Successful teamwork requires effective leadership, you cannot build a team without it. To be a successful team builder, you must know and/or learn what it takes to be an effective team leader. The great majority of team players need to be directed in teamwork and leadership concepts, because leading a team effectively is not an easy task. Whether your team is in the service industry, a factory or professional work force, a religious congregation, the sports world, the junior high school student council or more informal settings such as a summer camp or even your own family, team development must begin with the person in charge.

It also should be emphasized that teamwork is not a fad, it is not new. So, what is it?

By my definition: Teamwork is the activity of a group of individuals, united by a common purpose, who cooperate to achieve a common goal—a process known to produce unusually high-quality results.

A team leader is a person who helps others to maximize their potential and to do their best in reaching a common goal.

I set out on this study to learn from people who I believe offer a dynamic illustration of legendary team leadership and whose success is in

6

direct proportion to their ability to develop teamwork. The reason for my choice of basketball leaders exclusively is twofold: The size of the group most closely resembles the recommended number for teams in the workplace and basketball includes both sexes at the NCAA* playing level.

Collectively, the following men and women who shape this book have over 200 years experience in leading successful teams.

Dick Bennett,
Men's Basketball Coach,
University of Wisconsin-Green Bay

Alexander Gomelsky,
"Grandfather of Russian Basketball"

Don Nelson,
Head Coach, Golden State Warriors,
Oakland, California

Pat Head Summitt,
Women's Basketball Coach,
University of Tennessee-Knoxville

Judith M. Sweet,
Director of Athletics,
University of California-San Diego

Tara VanDerveer,
Women's Basketball Coach,
Stanford University, Stanford, California

John Wooden,
Retired Men's Basketball Coach,
University of California-Los Angeles

The knowledge they share is basic and straightforward; their philosophies are powerful.

I learned from these women and men that developing team leadership skills is a process which does not end; it is a personal journey that no one can prescribe, and there are no quick fixes or microwave recipes. Finding and presenting the primary elements of team leadership as practiced by these prominent team leaders was my goal. But I did not expect to discover a clear base of agreement on leadership principles from people with such different personalities, backgrounds and experiences.

My original plan was to offer you—potential and working team leaders and players—an introduction to teamwork and leadership concepts according to my experience; a biographical sketch of and interview with each participant focusing on their knowledge, philosophy and style, and finally an analysis that would integrate the information gathered and make it easy to index their leadership ideas and skills.

However, what you now see is the result of honing more than 300 pages of transcripts from two years of interviews, study and writing that changed the original concept and produced:

EIGHT FUNDAMENTAL ELEMENTS OF EFFECTIVE TEAM LEADERSHIP

These fundamental elements: BALANCE, RE-SPECT, LOVE, VISION, EXPECTATIONS/ROLE DEFINITION, WILLINGNESS TO BE LED, COMMITMENT TO CONTINUOUS IM-PROVEMENT, STRIVE TO BE YOUR BEST, can be posed as questions to any team leader wanting to examine his/her skills and effectiveness; they are meant to be a guide in your leadership development process.

I have applied these eight elements in my work with the very young—sixth through eighth graders—and the not so young, but highly experienced executives in corporate America. All eight elements are essential to successful team leadership. If any element is absent there will be a negative impact. Although each element is critically important and they are interdependent, I believe that balance holds the key to implementation of the other seven. If a leader is out of balance for the long term, he/she cannot be truly successful; without balance, your best will be elusive.

I hope this book serves as an inspiration and a resource to those who are, or would like to be, team leaders striving to make a difference in their team performance. This is not a "how-to" book; it is a primer for effective team leadership, and it will help to guide you in answering questions, [i.e., Which element is not in place?] when projects go awry or problems appear.

I do believe if you focus your learning on these eight fundamental elements your understanding of teamwork and its leadership will increase dramatically, as will your team's success.

Best wishes for a lifelong journey in effective team leadership.

WENDY WOODIN PECHE with
PAT GRAY THOMAS

Understanding the importance of "Balance," and knowing that its absence is often obvious and potentially dangerous, can begin at any age.

"In a junior high school leadership training workshop, a majority of the participants, when asked to rank the eight fundamental elements according to their degree of difficulty, thought that 'balance' would be 'the biggest challenge or the hardest element to achieve.'

"At the same time they decided, 'It's easy to see;' when someone does not have 'balance,' ... 'they yell and scream at you for making any kind of mistake; nothing is good enough; they are on you all the time.' "

W. W. Peche

Balance

Balance is the first element required for effective team leadership. It is marked by maturity, self-knowledge and inner security. It is the act of being stable and consistent; it keeps perspective in place, it creates energy and order.

Balance is not gained and automatically retained; it requires continual examination:

> *"I am always struggling with balance*
> *… I make the mistake that most*
> *coaches make, anybody in the*
> *position of leadership does it, I take it*
> *home. Sometimes it consumes me. I*

*have to back off ... to remind myself
that coaching is not number one; I
realize my faith and my family clearly
need to be the most important things
in my life ... Early in my career I taught
on the high school level. I explored the
ideas of great authors such as
Melville, Twain and Hawthorne; that
put me in touch with the wisdom that
allowed me to conclude the right
stuff."*

Bennett

*"It [balance] helps you keep your
temper and emotions under control—
otherwise you get out-coached."*

Wooden

Emotional control helps maintain consistency.
It is easy to smile and be happy when you per-
form well or belong to the winning team. But,

*"... when a leader is balanced, you
are the same person whether you are
winning or losing or things aren't
going your way."*

VanDerveer

Maturity and inner security are equally impor-

14

tant facets of balance. These components are built with self-acceptance and a deep sensitivity to others; you must know your own history and you must know what influenced you.

> *"A leader has to be secure ... as a person, which only comes from a sense of balance, to accept others' ideas."*
>
> Nelson

> *"Your goal is an inner strength and togetherness that is solid and secure in who you are and then things don't seem to shake you up as easily."*
>
> VanDerveer

> *"You must know yourself well enough to understand how you got to where you are."*
>
> Bennett

Another part of balance is an ability to give to yourself, and that must come before you can give to others:

> *"People who are not happy with themselves are not readily capable of giving a lot to others."*
>
> VanDerveer

15

At the same time, personal balance fosters, enjoys and shares a fun factor:

> *"It's important to have a sense of humor ... When I am balanced, I have a sense of humor and can laugh at myself."*
>
> Sweet

In addition, leadership requires a lot of energy. And balance helps to give you that energy:

> *"I take care of myself, work out, do things to make sure I have a lot of energy to be the best that I can be."*
>
> VanDerveer

An effective team leader also must be careful to extend the criteria for personal balance to all team players:

> *"As a coach looks for balance among team members—never selecting on talent alone—they [the players] must have balance in their lives."*
>
> Nelson

Personal balance, the first and most important element for effective team leadership, ultimately guarantees that an effective team leader has order in and a perspective on life; and this combination communicates that there is more to life than winning the next game, there is more to life than making your team players do it your way.

JOHN WOODEN'S
SEVEN-POINT CREED

Upon his graduation from eighth grade, John Wooden's father gave this poem to him.

"Making the Most of One's Self"

Be true to yourself.

Make each day your masterpiece.

Help others.

Drink deeply from good books.

Make friendship a fine art.

Build a shelter against a rainy day.

Pray for guidance and give thanks for your blessings every day.

Author unknown

Accepting imperfections is necessary for building "Respect."

"I have always chosen people with sufficient skill and talent, but also [those who] demonstrate tremendous character. ... A lot of my players don't [have] the greatest backgrounds and yet they have been given or developed character. ... [We are] going to struggle initially, we always have, but they are not going to give up. It is almost sequential in the way things develop.

"Once you succeed with this formula, getting good solid people who rank well across the board, others in the field think you are now going to get the great athletes. But the formula doesn't change; we still do not recruit off that top 100 list across the country. We continue to get the same kind of kids that put us here in the first place; it's character that makes the difference."

D. Bennett

Respect

Respect, the second element demanded of an effective team leader, is the act of honoring or showing high regard for the opinion, wishes and judgment of others; it builds bridges and creates teamwork.

Respect is defined, given and shared in a number of ways:

> *"It means giving credit to others and recognizing that people work with me, not for me."*
>
> Wooden

> *"It tells me to treat people the way I*

*want to be treated. ... That helps me
to be an example of a leader [the
players] want to follow. If they respect me and I respect them, we will
treat each other with respect."*

Summitt

*"It is a commitment to understanding
the views of those I work with."*

Sweet

*"Look for smart people who work
hard, believe in me and I believe in
them. Too, there must be honesty
and trust."*

Gomelsky

To encourage the best work from all group
members, a leader must earn their respect. To
gain this element you have to study each position and its player.

In athletics or in business,

*"The leader ... needs to know every
job and be able to do every job.
When they are able to do all of that,
then [he/she] will have respect for
each one of those jobs. I don't believe you can be a true leader unless*

you are willing to do all of that."

Nelson

Part of knowing every job and every player has to include recognition of:

> *"... the right to be imperfect. ... I tell the players, 'You are going to be led by a very imperfect person. You have to be good enough, big enough to understand that there are going to be a lot of mistakes made.' It [accepting imperfection] is a cornerstone for building respect."*

Bennett

And when mistakes are made, the "good enough, big enough" team leader and players do not look for someone to blame, they look for the cause: Not who, but how.

When disagreement is evident, the effective team leader's goal is to express his/her thoughts, not to convince others that he/she is right and they are wrong.

The differences between individuals on a team can be monumental. However, these differences are valuable because they expand the

23

resources of the group. If two people working on a single project always agree, one of them is probably not needed. And if an entire team is built with similar talent there will be insurmountable complications.

A major priority in team building is to encourage the players to respect each other's differences and understand that they are essential.

> *"If I can get them to do that, they will automatically respect one another, and they will come together."*
>
> Bennett

While an effective leader must bring the team together, it is also necessary to treat every person differently:

> *"You have to constantly study your players and recognize that each one has a distinct personality. ... Some [people] think that to be impartial you must treat everybody alike. I say that the best way to show partiality is to keep everyone alike. We must try to give the individual the treatment they earn and deserve."*
>
> Wooden

24

One of the greatest challenges to effective team leadership is to find and give the players what they need, rather than what the leader needs or thinks the players need.

"Look for individual needs and develop those. You need a plan for each person."

Gomelsky

In order to define what is important to each player, a leader must know their weaknesses. When addressing weaknesses, problems or needs—whether criticizing or analyzing—restraint is in order:

"I don't raise my voice often. I think you can constructively have discussions about people's weaknesses without causing them to lose their dignity. ... I recognize that different individuals have different needs; consequently, they are going to have different motivational needs."

Sweet

"If I were critical of a player in front of his teammates, he might go into a shell and not contribute to his poten-

*tial. I've had other players that you
have to, more or less, get on them in
front of others. That motivates them
more."*

Wooden

Respect is a motivating factor. It inspires all
players to strive, to produce, to achieve their
best work.

*"... the goal is to get the best out of
each individual, because that is what
everyone is going to contribute."*

Wooden

When respect is established and all players are
able to give their best, an effective leader shares
control.

*"I think you say to yourself, 'I am
going to loosen the reins now and let
you do what I know you are capable
of doing.'"*

Summitt

The sharing of control is the definitive result
of respect between player and leader. Trust
and loyalty are evident in this action:

*"... you know they [team members]
respect you ... they can trust you and
they will be loyal to you."*

Summitt

Shared respect, trust and loyalty create a successful team. Whether in business or in sports, for fame or for profit, team players produce exceptional results. On the professional basketball court where million-dollar contracts are involved, people assume it's harder, or that the players present different problems. But,

"Coaching at the NBA level isn't
harder. I never thought of it as a
problem because I respect the players, and that comes through. If the
respect is there, it doesn't matter if a
player is making $3 million or
$150,000 [the minimum contract],
he is going to try to do his best."*

Nelson

A final and necessary part of respect is developed away from work in a social environment; it is directly related to the quality of our communication and our relationships. Although building relationships is difficult in this frenetic, pressurized world, team members need to know each other as people rather than just team-mates or colleagues. Making the time to gather with co-workers outside the workplace is as important to the team's success as the planning sessions on the job.

"It is important for them to have fun together."

Sweet

Whether at a local cafe for midnight coffee, on the basketball court, in the corporate boardroom or the data processing department, when communication is at its best and you ask, "What does teamwork teach about life?" a simple answer is repeatedly heard:

"It teaches people respect, thank you, and respect."

Gomelsky

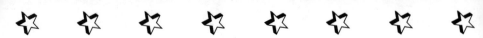

"Love" and/or "Caring" does not change with the score of a game or the end of a project.

"I got a lot of 'love' and attention and affection from my parents, grandparents, my aunts and uncles, and I feel like I have a battery that has a lot of voltage in it. I am capable of giving a lot to other people.

"What means the most to me? When the people I coach are happy when I call them; [they] write to me; things that are ... personal, those are the things that are real important to me."

T. VanDerveer

Love

Love is the third element necessary for effective team leadership. If **love** is too strong, as many leaders will insist, you can substitute **care**. This basic and simple element is shared by all team players at all levels and in many forms:

> *"... the job starts with me caring about the people I work with; and my number one job as a coach or leader is the morale of our team and their camaraderie."*

VanDerveer

"When you say love, you care; you share and you are considerate. ... If you don't have love, things get out of whack."

Wooden

"Love, to me, is a form of unselfishness. If you are uncomfortable with the word love, then I'll say caring— and you need every member of your team to know you really care about them."

Bennett

"It's knowing what's important to you, and you knowing what's important to me."

Summitt

When people care about each other, there is an understanding that they both will win:

"I like to see people who are able to give to others ... to extend themselves. The people that I coach, that I work with, give so much to me."

VanDerveer

"Many of my boys are [like] family. If

he [a player] has a problem at home, the wives, they call me; [they say] 'Father, speak [to] my husband.' You need good cooperation and communication, COMMUNICA-TION."

Gomelsky

Caring, paired with good communication, makes a leader want to acknowledge the contributions and the value of each team member:

"It's important to reward people who are producing and let them know how much you value them. THANK YOU is sometimes all that's needed."

Sweet

Whatever the terminology, team leadership always includes the expression of interest and concern; an effective team leader cares deeply and it is obvious and sincere:

"When you are working with others ... you really have to care and share in a way that lets people know that you are very sincere."

Wooden

Caring and its expression helps both leader and players to solve their problems. In our world of "star players," a careful sensitivity to interpersonal dynamics enables a team leader:

> *"... to take the jealousy out of sports and business. As long as the team wins, you don't want anybody to be jealous of another person's ability to make money or score or whatever it might be. You have to root for each other and pull each other up all the time."*
>
> Nelson

Caring makes it possible for an effective leader to expect the best, to expect success, from all team players.

> *"I have been around people who really care about me and have helped me. I am not able to work in environments that are not this way ... [environments] that I would describe as very cold."* As a result, *"I really try working with people; to be really positive, to focus on the good things they are doing. Also, because I care, I want to be critical in a way [that*

does] not accept anything but their best efforts and a positive attitude."

VanDerveer

"It is important when you hire some-one that you do everything you can to help [that person] be successful. If you hire people you really care about, you want to do this."

Sweet

"It is important in the business com-munity to take care of the people who take care of us; we sometimes forget that. My secretary has been with me for 16 years and that's not by accident."

Summitt

"Many people feel that what they do is unimportant, that no one cares how they get their job done. ... You have to really work hard to make people feel good about themselves so they can be successful."

VanDerveer

To help each player achieve success, an effec-tive team leader recognizes the many dimensions in every player's life:

> *"The person, the student, the athlete,*
> *all are considered equal."*
>
> Summitt

In order to help team players, you must be willing to extend yourself, to place yourself in the player's position:

> *"It's a natural result of what happens*
> *when people care. I look at myself*
> *and say, 'Would I be someone that I*
> *would want to play for?'"*
>
> VanDerveer

A team leader also understands:

> *"You cannot judge from a distance;*
> *you have to be close and help*
> *people help themselves."*
>
> Wooden

It is your responsibility as a team leader to know how to show you care based on each player's needs. Some prefer quiet appreciation, a note of praise or a private conversation; others want a more public announcement of achievement.

Knowing you care is not enough unless the team members know it too:

> *"Although he didn't always agree with us, he loved us."*

[A compliment to Wooden, from an unnamed player.]

Dick Bennett's note to his players
after a winning season:

LOVE[1]
BY KAHLIL GIBRAN

But let there be spaces in your togetherness,
And let the winds of the heavens
   dance between you.

Love one another, but make not a bond of love:
Let it rather be a moving sea between
   the shores of your souls.
Fill each other's cup but drink not from one cup.
Give one another of your bread but eat not
   from the same loaf.
Sing and dance together and be joyous,
   but let each one of you be alone,
Even as the strings of a lute are alone
   although they quiver with the same music.

Give your hearts, but not into each other's keeping.
For only the hand of Life can contain your hearts.
And stand together yet not too near together;
For the pillars of the temple stand apart,
And the oak tree and the cypress grow
   not in each other's shadow.

*When I saw this poem I thought
of our team. I like the togetherness
but I also like the independence.
   See if you agree.*

38   *Coach*

Belief in a purpose with a clear mental "Vision" is the beginning of team success.

"Winning the 1988 Olympic Gold Medal, this was my dream. I kept telling the boys, 'You do your best, you can win and beat the U.S., I know we can do it.' No one else believed me at first, but we did it."

A. Gomelsky

Vision

Vision, the fourth fundamental element, enables a team leader to see in the imagination that something ordinary or extraordinary can be accomplished. An effective team leader knows that success is attainable only if a clear mental picture, *"the dream,"* is in place.

"The dream" is the masterpiece that supplies answers to the **what** of purpose and the **how** of achievement. A vision includes,

> *"... [being] responsible for laying the foundation of the organization,*

*helping to put it all in place; it is
looking long range rather than being
concerned with what is going to
happen in the first year."*

Summitt

Looking long-range,

*"I feared so much [when moving up to
NCAA Level 1, at the University of
Wisconsin-Green Bay] until I got this
picture in my mind of what we could
do. I envisioned ... a level of quality at
this institution, in the basketball
forum, that would earn respect.
Everyone thinks in terms of wins or
losses; the media does a lot of that, so
do fans. But most leaders, most
coaches, think in terms of quality. ...
We could legitimately play quality
basketball and that was my vision, and
that's the one I shared. [I knew] if we
played this team defense ... we would
achieve quality."*

Bennett

And once the picture is clear,

"Team leaders need to sell the dream

42

... We must have everybody seeing this vision and caring about what we are doing; our strength is our togetherness." That includes the players who are unable to be major contributors, but still care about and share the dream. *"The success that we have enjoyed, every step along the way, has been for everybody."*

Bennett

The power that results from a shared vision builds cooperation and relationships, prevents internal competition, minimizes often disruptive attention to unimportant issues and engenders an understanding that team success belongs to every player equally:

"We get everyone thinking in the same direction and cooperating with each other, agreeing with each other and forming a kind of family. Everyone is happy with each other making decisions for the whole, not the individual."

Nelson

In sports and in business, all teams encounter problems that are potentially destructive:

*"There is so much competition,
especially in large companies; there is
fighting ... for credit, or ... they want
their department to be the best;
people don't see the big picture or
what it's all about, this is totally
contrary to the way it should be."*

Nelson

*"When everyone has the same vision,
you don't get caught up in the petty
things ... that really aren't important to
the big picture."*

VanDerveer

Success will be elusive if the players are not
convinced that each one of them has a vital
role. On the factory floor, the basketball court
or in council chambers,

*"It is critical that the leader make
everyone feel as if they are part of the
team, and that the successes
experienced by the team are the
results of everyone's combined
efforts."*

Nelson

The term *"combined efforts"* embraces every

44

level of an organization; it means that everyone participates:

> *"A company is doomed to fail if it feels that everyone needs to develop teamwork skills but management. Everyone is crucial to success—the twelfth man on the team or the president."*
>
> Nelson

An often forgotten factor that is essential to team success is the identification of individual and group strengths and weaknesses, and the subsequent setting of relationship or process goals. It must be remembered that teamwork is a process, and therefore subject to change. In 1981, when Summitt established the Definite Dozen [see page 62],

> *"... it was our expectation to be a winning team. But, I changed it, and our vision became what it takes to be successful."*
>
> Summitt

> *"Teams must be willing to continually assess themselves in relation to their team goals."*
>
> VanDerveer

45

A team leader always needs to study, to learn:

> "... to take a good look at what you are all about; how can you produce a level of quality that will earn the respect of the people you deal with. I would also pay close attention to the kinds of people ... who are helping you to reach the dream."
>
> Bennett

> "At the beginning of every year, the [University of California-San Diego] coaches establish their goals. I review [these goals] with them, and we try to make sure they are not setting goals that are unattainable and setting them up for failure."
>
> Sweet

The opening anecdote for this element, taken from the interview with Alexander Gomelsky, is proof that vision does produce legendary victories. Another example of the same quality:

In 1991, the Stanford University women's basketball team was told:

46

"We are going to take this team, as a very young team, and this will be a national championship team someday. Because we believe in it—we know how to do it—we are going to mold it."

VanDerveer

The Stanford Cardinals won the NCAA championship again in 1992.

How effective is your team and its vision? [See page 48.]

HOW EFFECTIVE IS YOUR TEAM?

COMMUNICATION
Are your meetings focused on relevant issues?
Do people know their responsibilities?
Are decisions effectively carried out by the team?
Are differences and conflicts openly addressed?
Is consensus decision-making used whenever possible?
Do team members participate in making decisions that
    affect their jobs and each other?
Is everyone encouraged to participate?

PURPOSE
Are team goals committed to by team members?
Are all members involved in achieving the team's goals?
Are priorities clear and derived from team objectives?
Are responsibilities/expectations defined and adhered to?
Do job responsibilities/expectations conflict?
Are conflicting job expectations openly discussed and
    resolved?

RESPECT
Is everyone aware of the strengths each member brings
    to the team?
Is work characterized by a high degree of cooperation?
Are members encouraged to make individual
    contributions to the team?
Are members responsible for doing their part?
Are team members respected for their competence?
When times get tough, do people pull together?
Do members feel a sense of work accomplishment and
    satisfaction?
Do members feel their time and energy is well spent?
Do team members work together efficiently?

Why is team assessment important?
1). All teams need to assess both their strengths and weaknesses.
2). An action plan can be developed to focus its learning and
    improve team performance.
3). A team can measure and celebrate its success.

"Roles and Expectations" must be clear with lines of communication always open to question and change.

"I played basketball three years for Dick Bennett, at Eau Claire [Wisconsin] Memorial High School. My senior year we were in the state tournament, and I hoped to be in the starting lineup for our first game. But the other forward was chosen. We won the tournament; I played in most of the games, and shortly after I asked the coach, 'Why didn't you choose me to play in the opener?'"

Bennett answered: "I didn't think you cared, if you had come to me then with your question, I would have let you start, figuring that you really wanted it. The same thing happened to me when I was in college; that is why I stress to every player, from the beginning, come to me with your questions."

Timothy Richman
Executive Director of Rehabilitation Institutes
Covenant Healthcare, Inc., Milwaukee

Defining
roles

Defining roles and expectations, the fifth fundamental element, is the first step in team orientation. For every leader and player there must be a clear statement and understanding of what each team member is to do and what it takes for each team member to succeed.

> *"Every coach has to structure the environment to foster teamwork."*
>
> Sweet

> *"Know your team leadership philosophy and what qualities you are looking for in your players and*

prioritize them."

Choosing team players is complicated and personal no matter what group or what the project. While all basketball coaches look for players with outstanding physical skills, they also seek mental sharpness and character traits that are of equal or greater importance:

> *"We look at the three A's: academic and athletic ability and attitude. We try to expose our program and its facets to student athletes so that they know we have a lot of discipline here. We are committed to hard work and [let them know] they are going to have to perform and to perform at a certain level."*
>
> Summitt

> *"I look for self-motivators ... players who are dedicated and focused, with a single-mindedness and a desire to win; who are willing to set aside some of their skill for the team. A guy who is a scorer may be asked to defend or pass. He has to be willing to do that. The team becomes the most important*

52

part of everyone's job. If the team is successful and wins, everyone is happy. You can't be happy if the team loses and you have a good game. You shouldn't be happy when that happens; I clearly expect that from my players."

Nelson

"I like people who are intelligent, who work very hard and get the job done ... who believe in me ... who believe in them [each other]. ... [A player] must be patient and in good communication."

Gomelsky

"I am looking for people who want to be the best they can be ... someone who takes pride in doing the right thing and doing it the right way; someone who strives for excellence and recognizes that the job is never done, and they are not dissatisfied as a result; someone who cares about other people and is sensitive to their co-workers ... one who is team oriented and willing to put forth whatever effort is necessary, while not compromising principles."

Sweet

"I tend to look for the more unspectacular skills. The willingness to do the little things; to be a smart player, to have a degree of mental toughness. I especially look for an unselfish character; unselfishness is what any team must have as its undergirding. I choose people who demonstrate tremendous character— work habits, attitudes, intelligence— for the game. I look for people who don't want the splashy approach, are not going to quit or take the easy way out."

Bennett

"I want quickness under control; that means you have balance—physical, mental and emotional balance. It's important that you get [players] to lose [themselves] in the group for the good of the group."

Wooden

"I look at basketball skills, work habits and attitudes, all three must be in

balance. I enjoy working most with
great attitudes and great work habits;
[with these] I would go with lower
skills. I am uncomfortable working with
someone who is very skilled, but has
poor work habits and a poor attitude. I
am not interested in coaching people
that are me-me-me."

VanDerveer

Once the decision is made—the player fits—
role definition builds a sense of belonging; it
leads players to recognize their part, and its
necessity, in the achievement of team goals.

"There are different roles that must be
played, and I try to get across that no
role is more important than another ...
we are all working toward the same
goal."

Wooden

Defining roles and expectations can cause
difficulties:

"... Reality hits when you're in a
business or program where
competitors are equally talented.
Some cannot handle that, some can't

play a role, we start talking about
being respectful to other people."

Summitt

Along with respect and role responsibility that may need examination and strengthening, it is obvious that role flexibility is critical. "It's not my job," is an unacceptable cliche in a team-oriented environment.

It's a smart team leader who remembers:

"When I drafted on talent, looking the other way regarding character, I have been burned almost every time."

Nelson

In business, roles are defined in relation to: problem solving, conflict resolution, sharing information, development of policy and procedure, crisis management, communication. But, a job description is not the answer to role definition; it is most often vague and merely provides a title that frequently is or becomes inconsistent with team goals.

Roles need to be reconsidered on a regular basis, with or without change in expectations or goals. It is especially important before and during organizational changes and big projects

56

to immediately inform players, solicit feedback and encourage discussion regarding the clarity of roles.

The importance of defining roles and expectations is further heightened by helping to simplify the evaluation process:

> *"Defining roles and expectations means that you know what you will be evaluated on. We evaluate effort and execution."*
>
> Summitt

> *"The number one goal at all times [is] a positive attitude; without that I would write on the player's card, 'Your attitude is counter productive to our team's success, come talk to me,' or, 'You make a change—see a counselor, do something—or you are going to be gone.' "*
>
> VanDerveer

> *"It's very important to have team players to work with. I have assumed some responsibility when I hire somebody. If I find they are falling short I try to work with them to take*

*care of the shortcomings. If, after
several opportunities, [he/she]
continues to be disruptive or not
contributing to the team and its
members, I would suggest they would
be happier some place else."*

Sweet

It is not easy to evaluate, but it is necessary. An effective team leader must give players honest, accurate, compassionate feedback so they will accept the evaluation and improve.

Effort and execution are valid evaluation criteria for any group. But, often problems can be eliminated before they begin. An effective leader presents a clear philosophy and describes exactly what the players can expect. And the potential team member should decide whether the fit is right or wrong before the final decision is made:

*"I think when people have a problem,
it's because they have been misled."*

Summitt

Another problem that arises in teamwork is a loss of confidence or loss of the team vision. How does a team leader handle this situation?

58

"I try to go out of my way to take some extra time to find out how they feel and to help them analyze what's happening and why. It's important to understand the realities of when you should be successful and when you may not succeed; when not to be too hard on yourself and when you are in an environment where there are factors over which you have no control."

Sweet

In business, all too often leaders do not explain what they want until the employee fails to produce the desired result or performance.

"I say to my players from day one, 'If there is a problem or something you need to know, don't discuss it among yourselves, come to me directly.' We must have direct one-on-one communication. Unfortunately, very few people do it."

Bennett

It's a common problem:

"People have a real hard time speaking up for what they need and want. I am not the top of the pyramid, I have a boss that I report to. I need to tell the people that I coach what I want, but I have to do the same for the person I work for."

VanDerveer

There is a direct correlation between the effectiveness of your communication and the effectiveness of your relationships. Your goal as an effective team leader is to develop and foster positive relationships through direct and open communication. To exemplify your communication expectations: create an open environment that encourages conversation; acknowledge and thank your staff for stating their concerns, whether you agree or not; listen closely and do not interrupt; do not respond in a defensive or judgmental tone, and follow up on your or their response and suggestions promptly.

"Clear roles and expectations are the result of good one-on-one communication."

Summitt

60

In conclusion,

"The most important thing in the development of a basketball team is to have your players team-oriented, and not just on the basketball court."

Wooden

Off the court or in the business world,

"We may not invest as much time as we should in bringing the right person into the program. But once they are hired, we are responsible for helping them to be successful in the same way that a coach is responsible for making sure that [each] team member is going to fit and help the team to be successful."

Sweet

LADY VOLUNTEERS
DEFINITE DOZEN

To Stay Here:
Be Responsible
Be Respectful
Be Honest
Be Loyal

To Play Here:
Commit to Work Hard
Commit to Becoming a Smart Player
Put the Team Before Yourself
Have a Winning Attitude

To Be Successful Here:
Be Coachable and Communicate
With Your Coaches and Teammates;
Have Great Leaders, Eager Followers and
Role Players;
Influence Your Opponent;
Be Consistently Motivated
and Play With Confidence

Summitt's expectations for her players.

Team leadership demands that you are "Willing to be led."

"If I recruit ... people [with] the talent and the skill [for the open] position; if I know I've done my part in training and preparing, then why not let them go. You have to take away that control factor; that's very hard to do because ... I tend to be very structured. ... probably the best thing I did ... to loosen [control] is realize that I wasn't a great recruiter. ... about eight years ago I hired ... the best recruiting coordinator possible. ... I said, 'You do it, you organize it and you coach me. You tell me what to do.' She is great."

P. Head Summitt

Willingness
to be led

A willingness to be led is the sixth fundamental element demanded for effective team leadership. In teamwork, leader and players act together; the contribution of each participant is of equal value, and consummate success is possible only if a leader accepts these precepts and is able to share the decision-making and/or relinquish control [when it benefits the team].

An effective team leader knows:

> *"When we control everyone or everything, we may produce good results but not commitment. Without commitment the results will never be*

as high or effective as they are with commitment."

Wooden

"As a leader, you have to let go of the control factor; let players do what you've trained them to do, what they have the skill to do. The advantage in basketball is the coach can't physically play the game once the whistle blows."

Summitt

This is a difficult concept for many beginning team players. The common acceptance of knowledge and guidance from a single authority figure makes teamwork—and its leadership principles—troublesome for those steeped in traditional business programs. But,

"I doubt that it's more effective to independently make decisions ... It's really important for me to regularly get input from the people that I work with, to find what they think is or is not working; and if it's not working, what their suggestions are for making it better."

Sweet

66

Turning to others for suggestions illustrates clearly:

"People work with you, not for you," and it denotes *"... being more concerned with finding the best way, not your way."*

Wooden

In seeking the best way,

"I tell team members, 'You have to take responsibility for the success of our team. If we are depending totally on me and my brain, we are in trouble. I don't pretend I always have the best ideas. ... More than anything [in my career], I have really learned a lot from the players I coach; I try to really listen to things they say."

VanDerveer

"If you listen to them, they are far more apt to listen to you."

Wooden

Good leaders know that good ideas come from listening. It is listening with acceptance that expresses a willingness to be led, and that pro-

67

duces a dedicated team:

> *"Appreciate the fact that you cannot lead without eager followers."*
>
> Summitt

If you, a friend or a team member questions your willingness to be led or learn from others, have someone [or do it yourself] time your speaking versus your listening during a group problem-solving meeting. You will find it a revealing experience.

Good communication is paramount to effective leadership, and it is apparent that it involves far more than talking. The interaction between leader and players is an opportunity to teach and encourage players to make their own decisions:

> *"You train [players] to make the proper decisions at the proper time, and then you have to honor them by giving them the right to do it."*
>
> Nelson

At the same time,

> *"We also learn from the athlete who*

68

plays the game physically, mentally and emotionally; it is not beyond me to go in at halftime and say, 'What do you think?'"

Summitt

"I am always trying to get my players to come up with ideas. The more they feel comfortable doing that, the more they respond, and you find that they have the best ideas. They are the ones out there playing the game."

Nelson

"You have to feel secure in your own person to accept the ideas of others and use them if you can, and give credit to those who do it [give suggestions].

"Do not take credit for yourself, feel good about sharing that."

Nelson

A leader is often seen as **the** powerful entity. Paradoxically, it is followers who give a leader this power; the followers are **the team**, they will stay together and they will work together as long as their ideas are accepted and valued.

"... 25 to 30 years ago, I was a dictator. I taught the same every night: 'Listen to me and don't talk.' But sometimes I make mistakes; I lose good players because there is no communication for them."

Gomelsky

For ten years, Gomelsky acted as, in his terms, "a dictator"; then,

"I don't like it; I think ... boys who communicate, who work hard play very well. [Following this realization], I [am] close friend [to players]; boys took me [as] father. ... Before practice, in practice, I help boys. We communicate together. I ask, 'What [is] your opinion of this exercise?' Because I communicate, I look for better exercise for them. I study."

Gomelsky

Many people in sports and business,

"... work at having strong leaders and eager followers." In reality, *"It's the followers who make this whole thing work."*

Summitt

70

Rarely does an effective team leader have a player who wants the impossible. The major request is to have a voice that is heard and valued. Although all the decisions are not going to be made by the group, players should be certain of a part in the decision-making process, particularly when it affects team goals, their jobs or the policies they have to enforce. An effective team leader is an astute listener and he/she learns and understands the needs, ideas and issues of all players; if their needs are not met or dealt with, the job and the organization will suffer.

"Commitment to Continuous Improvement" assures growth and flexibility.

"I talk it all the time. If I coach, I study. I like to go to ballet. ... In Germany, I think and I go to ballet. ... When I am in Joliet, [Illinois], I go to ballet. I watch ballet in Russia. I look and ... I think maybe I use.

"All [the] time I think maybe this combination [is] good. Sometimes at night I get up, [look] in basketball books and write new combination. ... If coach finishes study, he [is] finished. If I not interested in study, goodbye."

A. Gomelsky

Commitment
to continuous
improvement

A commitment to continuous improvement, the seventh fundamental element of effective team leadership, is based on the belief that every person needs and wants to build on and improve the skills he/she brings to the group. Therefore, an effective team leader, knowing that team building and teamwork is an unending process, is always working to improve; always looking for growth opportunities; always analyzing strengths and weaknesses, and watching for problems.

"Continuous improvement is about being patient and persistent, and

constantly wanting to do better. You
must strive for excellence, and
recognize the job is never done."

Sweet

To ensure improvement, you must want to excel:

"You must be willing to pay the price,
and that doesn't just happen by
showing up; it demands constant
striving to be better."

VanDerveer

What makes this commitment so basic, so important? The certainty that,

"A team that wins rebounds, wins the
game."

Gomelsky

While this concept is a truism for Russian basketball stars/winners, in teamwork it means more than having the tallest players; winning and success depend on an ability to turn around, change pace and go in new directions. And a commitment to continuous improvement promises the needed flexibility and openness to new ideas; a willingness to do what is necessary to accomplish the task.

74

However, it is not possible to have improvement or growth and change without conflict. And the only response to this inevitability is:

> *"Don't let conflict settle in; anticipate it, deal with it and develop strategies to cope with it."*
>
> Sweet

> *"The way I try to handle most of the conflicts ... is by creating leaders within the team. The leadership structure—captains or veterans or whatever—pass down the problem solving. If you can talk to your leaders within the group, before [the problems] manifest themselves into something major ... you handle them before they are blown out of proportion."*
>
> Nelson

Conflict never comes at a good time, so be ready:

> *"I think it is like preparing for a flat tire; practice changing a tire before it happens. Talk to other people to get*

*insights ... get their ideas on how to
solve problems and then put together
your own plan."*

VanDerveer

An effective team leader must remember that diversity, an absolute necessity in teamwork, is often at the base of conflict; it is manifested through ego, idiosyncrasies, jealousy, someone not carrying their fair share. Or that is the perception. It follows immediately that a big problem is the tendency to think the conflict, given time, will solve itself.

*"I try not to let it settle in. I discuss it
with the individual or those involved to
understand why the conflict exists,
identify a solution or work out a
remedy. The real challenge is to nip it
in the bud."*

Sweet

On the basketball court, if conflict arises or expectations are not met, it's easy.

*"[When] a player begins to believe he
is bigger than the team, the coach has
the greatest ally: the bench."*

Wooden

Does the business world or any team leader have or need an equivalent to "the bench"? No, the bench is replaced with time taken to discuss the problem. Although there is agreement that ego is the greatest challenge to building a team, it also is almost always evident when conflict arises that expectations have not been clearly stated. It must be stressed early and often that in teamwork group needs and goals outweigh those of any individual.

> *"There may be five stars, but there is only one ball."* [Said in reference to the vulnerability of the 1992 U.S. Olympic Basketball Team.]
>
> Gomelsky

Commitment to continuous improvement also helps a team to learn from the hard times. All coaches are familiar with the struggle to rebuild:

> *"But, we do not give up. I give credence to the fact that there is a great deal learned during the hard times. In losing and failure there is perhaps more to be learned, if you are patient enough to learn [from] it."*
>
> Bennett

Patience is one of those common and essential, but elusive characteristics:

> *"Most of us don't have it. But, it takes time to build teams properly; worthwhile things take time and they should."*
>
> Wooden

There are different approaches to continuous improvement; what it looks like and how it can be nurtured. While utilizing individual strengths, it is necessary to encourage players to work on their weaknesses.

> *"On the basketball court, if my strength lies in shooting, that's great. The coach is going to give me the ball. But to perform up to expectations, I must develop my total game. I have to do more than just shoot the ball."*
>
> Summitt

It is imperative that team members are highly motivated to improve in all areas. Players must be willing to go the extra step, it is important for them to volunteer to:

> *"... take the extra assignments that*

strengthen their contribution as professionals."

Sweet

To make improvement possible, decision makers must be risk takers who are willing to offer players new opportunities.

"I would not be where I am now [in 1991 Sweet became the first woman elected to lead the NCAA] *if those who vote for the NCAA president, if those who choose athletic directors, were not willing to do something not done before."*

Sweet

An effective team leader understands the necessity for patience, the willingness of competitors to play to any weakness, that life's greatest teacher is experience and that mistakes—as the easiest experiences to remember—lead to improvement:

"We are working toward 100%: that's perfection. While I know we will not make it, I expect an effort toward that [goal]. *I expect a willingness to work harder, because we can always improve."*

Wooden

79

I THANK MY COMPETITORS

My competitors do more for me
than my friends.

My friends are too polite to point out my
weaknesses, but my competitors go to great
expense to tell of them.

My competitors are efficient and diligent.
They make me search for ways to improve
my products and services.

My competitors would take my business away
from me if they could.

This keeps me alert to hold what I have.

If I had no competitors, I would be lazy,
incompetent and complacent. I need the
discipline they enforce upon me.

I thank my competitors.
They have been good to me.

God Bless Them All.
Author unknown

Summitt: *"I carry this with me all the time."*

To "Strive to Be Your Best" is to play against perfection or against the game, not against an opponent.

"In the final round of the high school golf club championship, my opponent was a close friend and golfing partner since first grade. I remember trying so hard to beat her. After nine holes I was down 18 strokes. On the tenth hole, I decided she would probably win and I should relax and have some fun. Concentrating on my game, not my friend's, the next eight holes were mine. Tied at the 18th, I blew a birdie putt.

"But, I clearly remember my sense of pride in coming back to a one-stroke loss. I do not recall a coach ever telling me, 'Be the best that you can be.'"

W.W. Peche

S trive to be your best

The eighth and final element of effective team leadership takes form as a mandate: Strive to be your best wherever you are, whatever the project, and look beyond winning.

In striving to be your best,

> *"A person needs to be more interested in [his/her] own character than in [his/her] reputation; never try to be better than someone else, learn from others and never cease to be the best that you can be."*
>
> Wooden

To be an effective team leader:

"The most important thing to instill in staff or team members is 'wanting to be the best that you can be.'"

Sweet

To strive to be your best you must have personal aspirations based on your own talent, skill and ability to accomplish for yourself as well as for the team. In the same way, it is the responsibility of a team leader to understand and to help in the realization of each player's personal goals.

An effective team leader knows that achieving goals, whether personal or team goals, and coping with victory demands as much energy and the same learning process as recovering from losses. When the satisfaction level is high, that's when the questions begin. What's in it for me? Why work so hard? Where do we go now?

"When that happens, look out. People handle failure better than winning; once they win, they think there is no room or reason to improve."

Summitt

Once you have accomplished what you hoped for, it's not certain that past plans are always going to work. It is necessary to anticipate future obstacles and how to prevent them from interfering with long-range goals; remind yourself:

"Success is not an accident."

VanDerveer

"It is important to build on successful strategies."

Sweet

"There is no quick fix in any circumstance you encounter. You must be committed, in the long term, to make things happen."

Bennett

"Most teams actually self-destruct, as opposed to getting beaten by someone else."

VanDerveer

Team leaders and players must know or learn, in athletics and in business:

"People are fighting for credit rather

than just doing the best they can as individuals and as a whole."

Nelson

"If you lose your temper you are going to be outplayed. The smartest man I think I ever knew was my father. With only a high school education, he kept himself under control; I never heard him speak ill of another person, and I never heard him use profanity. I tell my players, 'No excessive jubilation or any excessive dejection; if you do your best, that's what counts.' "

Wooden

For all team players winning is a laudable and definitive group goal. Awards, championships and special recognitions are valuable in specific circumstances. But, a successful winner knows that although victory brings a boost in status, it is only a temporary elevation; it is only a small part of long-term growth and development:

"You like to win it [the NCAA championship] again. As much as I would like to win it again, I would love for someone else to feel it, because

*it's so great. Yes, we love winning,
and so you want it for the kids you're
coaching today ... but you also want it
for the other coaches that are really
your friends."*

VanDerveer

An effective team leader emphasizes that ex-
ternal competition helps the team to grow. The
opponent may be bigger or faster, smarter or
more experienced, but,

*"We ask no quarter and give none;
that means we play against the game
... not the opponent, not another
person. We don't expect them to feel
sorry for us or vice versa. We are out
there to do our best and that's what
it's all about."*

Bennett

Effective team leadership extends beyond team
goals. It requires you to look beyond winning:

*"Success can only be obtained
through self-satisfaction and knowing
you made the effort to become the
best of which you are capable. We
must be judged on how close we have*

come to reaching our own level of competency."

Wooden

Strive to be your best. It inspires and reflects a true team approach.

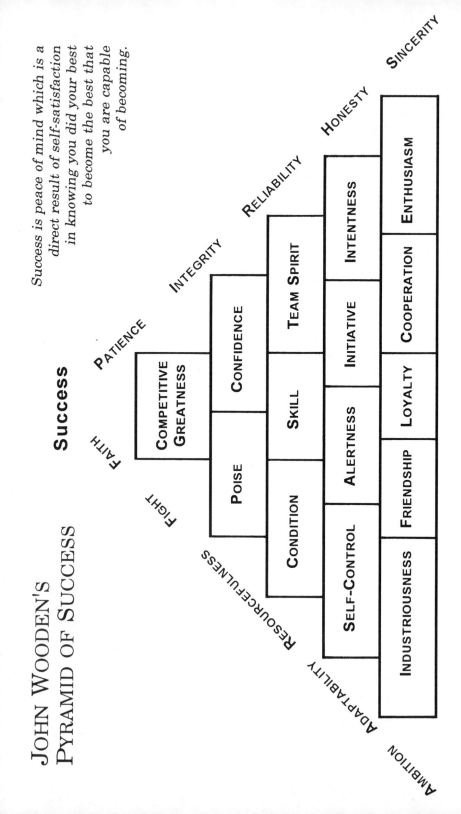

Competitive Greatness: Be at your best when your best is needed. Enjoyment of a difficult challenge.

Faith: Through prayer.

Patience: Good things take time.

Fight: Determined effort.

Integrity: Purity of intention.

Resourcefulness: Proper judgement.

Poise: Just being yourself. Being at ease in any situation. Never fighting yourself.

Confidence: Respect without fear. May come from being prepared and keeping all things in proper perspective.

Reliability: Creates respect.

Adaptability: To any situation.

Condition: Mental-Moral-Physical. Rest, exercise and diet must be considered. Moderation must be practiced. Dissipation must be eliminated.

Skill: A knowledge of and the ability to properly and quickly execute the fundamentals. Be prepared and cover every little detail.

Team Spirit: A genuine consideration for others. An eagerness to sacrifice personal interests of glory for the welfare of all.

Honesty: In thought and action.

Ambition: For the noble goals.

Self-Control: Practice self-discipline and keep emotions under control. Good judgement and common sense are essential.

Alertness: Be observing constantly. Stay open-minded. Be eager to learn and improve.

Initiative: Cultivate the ability to make decisions and think alone. Do not be afraid of failure, but learn from it.

Intentness: Set a realistic goal. Concentrate on its achievement by resisting all temptations and being determined and persistent.

Sincerity: Makes friends.

Industriousness: There is no substitute for work. Worthwhile results come from hard work and careful planning.

Friendship: Comes from mutual esteem, respect and devotion. Like marriage, it must not be taken for granted, but requires a joint effort.

Loyalty: To yourself and to all those depending upon you. Keep your self-respect.

Consideration: With all levels of your co-workers. Listen if you want to be heard. Be interested in finding the best way, not in having your own way.

Enthusiasm: Brushes off upon those with whom you come in contact. You must truly enjoy what you are doing.

Author's note

During the writing of this book, it was often suggested that readers might miss a precise answer for "how to" form and maintain a successful team. My response was always: Please remember that before teamwork begins you must have an effective leader.

That is why I chose to focus my efforts on leadership. When your purpose, your vision, is clear and your team is assembled; when individual skills and tasks are identified and understood; with a process for interaction formed, I firmly believe that the "how to" for teamwork is inherent in the eight fundamental elements.

However, recognizing the need to analyze, I offer the following guide.

ASSESSING YOUR LEADERSHIP DEVELOPMENT

BALANCE
Do I feel mentally, physically and spiritually balanced?

Are my emotions under control whenever and wherever problems arise?

Do I spend enough time with family, friends and interests outside of work?

Do I get the right exercise and the proper nutrition?

Are humor and laughter a part of everyday situations?

Do I feel energized and excited by challenge?

Is teamwork enjoyable?

RESPECT
Do my actions reflect my respect for each team member?

Do I prize the unique contributions of each player?

Do I understand each player's personal style; what he/she needs for recognition, support and to feel valued?

Am I honest and direct with all players?

Do team members openly acknowledge each other's talents?

Do I stress the importance of our differences?

LOVE
Do I really care about all team members?

Do I tell every player how important he/she is to the team?

Am I comfortable expressing my emotions?

Do players know that I care for them as individuals, beyond their team membership?

Do I always give credit for accomplishments and contributions?

Do I use **caring** confrontation to deal with conflict before individual or team issues get out of control?

VISION
Do I have a clear sense of purpose?

Is the purpose understood by the team?

Can team members describe our vision?

Do the players believe in and care about our purpose as much as I do?

Am I focused on the big picture or often distracted by details?

To keep the team focused, do I frequently discuss our purpose with the players, particularly when solving problems?

Do I speak with enthusiasm and commitment to our vision?

DEFINING ROLES
Have I clearly defined every role so the candidate can decide if he/she fits before joining the team?

Does everyone know what makes their role critical?

Have we, as a group, discussed each role to identify and resolve potential conflict?

Have I clearly stated my expectations for individual and team performance?

Do I give regular feedback on performance and address what falls short of expectations before problems get too big?

Do players understand that they are accountable for their performance?

Do players know how and on what they will be evaluated?

Does everyone understand how we measure success?

Do I reassess roles and expectations whenever needs change?

WILLINGNESS TO BE LED
Do I believe players have valuable ideas and do I seek their input?

Do I rephrase new ideas to help clarify their meaning?

Do I implement suggestions when possible or at least discuss why we have or have not acted on a proposal?

Do I always give credit to the author of an idea?

Do I encourage group discussion and avoid dominating team meetings?

Is the environment safe for disagreement with me?

COMMITMENT TO CONTINUOUS IMPROVEMENT
Do I continually question: How do we improve?

Are the players motivated to accomplish more than expected?

Are mistakes analyzed for opportunities?

Do we regularly set new goals?

Are we committed to success in the long run versus the immediate future?

Do I, do the players, have personal and team improvement plans?

STRIVE TO BE YOUR BEST
Do I praise individual effort regardless of team success or failure?

Do we celebrate our successes?

Do all players set goals that can change as his/her skill develops?

Do I promote collaboration rather than internal competition?

Have I stressed that the primary goal for a team player is to look beyond winning, to reach for perfection and your personal best?

Dick Bennett, University of Wisconsin-Green Bay basketball coach since 1985, believes that team building "... begins with the dream." And building teams is what this leader, born in Pittsburgh, Pennsylvania, April 20, 1943, has been doing in Wisconsin, at every level of amateur basketball for close to thirty years.

Raised and educated in Wisconsin at Clintonville High School and Ripon College, where he received a bachelor of arts in physical education, Bennett started coaching and teaching at West Bend High School in 1965.

In his years of coaching, as a winner of ten Coach-of-the-Year awards—on conference and national tournament levels—his coaching statistics and awards speak clearly of his leadership skills and his success:

1982 and 1985
       WSUC* Coach of the Year;

1984   NAIA* National Coach of the Year;

1985   NAIA Coach of the Year, District 14 and Area IV;

1990   NCAA Final Four, one of "The Most Underrated Coaches";

1990 and 1992
       Mid-Continent Conference Coach of the Year;

1992 and 1994
       Kodak/NABC* Coach of the Year, District 11.

In 11 years at five different high schools, Bennett posted a win-loss record of 168-60. After 18 years at the university level, his teams have won 339 games and lost 180. His 1984 University of Wisconsin-Stevens Point team lost the NAIA National Championship in overtime.

On another level of distinction, two of his university players are on NBA teams: Terry Porter, an NBA all-pro, is with the Portland Trailblazers, and Anthony Bennett, his son, is with the Charlotte Hornets.

The Bennett family includes another basketball career: daughter Kathi, a former all-state basketball player, is women's head basketball coach at the University of Wisconsin-Oshkosh. Offering support off the court is wife Anne, who also grew up in Clintonville, and youngest daughter Amy, a speech therapist for Cerebral Palsy, Inc., in Green Bay.

Always a three sport athlete [baseball, basketball and football] from high school in Clintonville, to Ripon College, Bennett won all-conference honors for the three years [freshmen were not eligible for varsity sports at that time] he competed in baseball and football, and as the sixth man on three straight championship basketball teams.

Bennett describes himself as "a builder," and considers the ability to sell the team concept, "the dream," his greatest strength as a coach. But also, he has a "good eye for talent" and is a master at choosing players with the character necessary to form a successful team. He believes that character, as much as or more than the initial talent needed to play the game, is what it takes to succeed over the long run. "People with character aren't going to give up," he said. "They have good work habits, a good attitude and intelligence for the game; they are decent people with good hearts."

Bennett grades himself as an "average at best" bench coach. However, along with his NCAA peers, who told the nation in 1990 Final Four competition that he was one of "The Most Underrated Coaches," other basketball pundits rank Bennett as one of the best teachers in basketball and as a defensive coach without equal.

Alexander Gomelsky, the "Grandfather of Russian Basketball," started his coaching career at age 19 with the 1947 Spartak Leningrad women's basketball team. A strong believer in the absolute necessity of study, which continues to fill his spare hours, his education reflects an early determination to succeed in the sports world:

1945-1948 Leningrad Coach's School;

1950-1953 Sports Institute of Leningrad;

1986 Ph.D., Moscow Academy of Sports.

Gomelsky describes the game of basketball as "my life," and he loves to relate his experience at the 1988 Olympics: "I know, United States basketball is best in the world ... but sometimes, I win."

He was the leader of five Olympic medal-winning basketball teams:

1960 and 1964, Silver;

1968 and 1980, Bronze;

1988, Gold.

From his first championship with the Army Sports Club of Riga, Latvia, where he coached men's basketball from 1953 to 1966, this born fighter thought of Olympic gold.

However, before the gold, 35 years of hard work produced a number of European, Soviet and world championship teams with the Central Army Sports Club of Moscow men's team [1966 to 1986], and the U.S.S.R. national men's team [1959 to 1970 and 1976 to 1988]:

1953-1985   Champion of the Soviet Union 15 times
             European Cup Competition Champion
             seven times;

1959-1987   European Champion nine times;

1959, 1967 and 1982   FIBA* World Champion.

Following the Seoul Olympics, Gomelsky coached a team in Spain, until he was called to serve as president of the U.S.S.R. Basketball Federation. However, it wasn't long before he discovered, "This is a job I do not like," and he moved to France, where he coached the Limoges Basketball team in 1990-1991.

Gomelsky arrived in the United States in 1991. Invited by High Five America, he also was excited to give his youngest son the opportunity to live and study here.

High Five America is a non-profit organization supported by major U.S. universities and committed to helping young people and adults make healthy choices in their confrontation with drugs and alcohol. Using athletes for positive role models and effective educational materials, High Five encourages drug-free living through basketball exhibition games, school assemblies, camps and drug education training seminars conducted in schools, churches and the work place.

In Russia, home is in Moscow; in the U.S., for Gomelsky, his wife, Lilia, and their youngest son, Kirill, home was in Skokie, Illinois, where his son Alexander, a Cornell University graduate, is now in the import-export business. Another son, Vladimir, is a television basketball commentator in Russia.

Wherever he travels, Gomelsky closely watches the NBA, he exercises and jogs every day, he studies the lives of famous coaches and, as an author, he continues to write.

Don Nelson, nicknamed Nellie, is general manager [since 1987] and head coach [since 1988] of the Golden State Warriors, Oakland, California. A 32-year veteran of the NBA, as a player and a head coach, Nelson holds the distinction of being a member of the most winning teams in the NBA's 49-year history. He also is one of only seven head coaches to reach 800 NBA victories and to lead teams ranked number one in both offense and defense.

Born May 15, 1940, and raised on his grandparents' farm in rural Sherrard, Illinois, Nelson went on to the University of Iowa, where as a

Hawkeye, he was twice an All-America selection and still ranks as the sixth-leading scorer in University of Iowa basketball history.

Nelson's professional basketball career started in 1962, as a player for the Chicago Zephyrs; he moved to the Los Angeles Lakers in 1963, and was signed by the Boston Celtics as a free agent in 1965. Many fans remember Nelson as the star sixth man for Boston, who made a stunning shot in the closing minutes of the seventh game of the 1969 World Championship series to give his team a 108-106 victory over the Los Angeles Lakers. In his years with the Celtics, they won five NBA titles.

Leaving Boston in 1976 to become head coach and vice president of basketball operations for the Milwaukee Bucks, Nelson started on his club record of 540-344. In eleven seasons with the Bucks, he led the team to 50 or more game wins in seven straight seasons for seven division titles; second only to Boston's streak of nine straight division wins.

For close to 20 years of coaching, Nelson has been highly respected and praised by his peers as a risk taker and a creative coach; by general managers for his extraordinary ability to judge talent and his rapport with the players; and by players for his style. In 1992, a random sampling of NBA players found Nelson the coach they would most like to play for.

Wary of terms such as "genius" or "great coach" or "the best coach in the NBA," Nelson once told *USA Today*, "I teach and I preach, but I don't overdo either. Having fun is important, too, but I can also be as tough as anybody. If the players know you like them, they can take it, and all of my players know that underneath everything I love them."

The only NBA coach to be named Coach of the Year three times [1983, 1985 and 1992], Nelson likes to be seen as he was when he was a player, "... not great at anything, but good in a whole lot of areas. He knows how to draft, cut deals, recognize talent, coach, make decisions and create a family atmosphere," said son Donn, a Warriors assistant coach. Nelson is known for popularizing "... the concept of versatility and interchangeable parts and a unique way of defending. He believes in disrupting. ... He has as many ways to disrupt an offense as you have number of plays," said Jim Lynam, general manager of the Washington Bullets.

True to his unpretentious demeanor, Nelson's awards and contributions are often off the record, but this is what we found:

1986   Nellie's Farm Fund—a charitable program to help needy Wisconsin farm families. Nelson raised more than $500,000 auctioning his famous fish ties and his taped-up coaching shoes while driving across the state on a farm tractor;

1990   Vincent T. Lombardi Champions Award—an annual presentation to a coach or athlete for significant civic contributions;

1992   All-Star coach of the West Team;

1994   Head coach of Dream Team II for the World Games in Toronto.

Alameda, California, is home to Nelson and wife Joy Wolfgram, who heads a charitable organization, Warriors Women Save Lives, that helps underserved breast cancer victims.

With a grown family—in addition to Donn there are daughters Chris and Katie—Nelson heads for the golf course in his spare time.

Pat Head Summitt, head coach of women's basketball at the University of Tennessee, Knoxville, since 1975, is the only women's coach with three NCAA titles: 1987, 1989 and 1991. She also is the only basketball coach, man or woman, to win an Olympic medal as a player [Silver in 1976] and as a coach [Gold in 1984]. And in the minds of many sports enthusiasts, her greatest achievement is the 100% graduation rate of her four-year players.

Born June 14, 1952, in Henrietta, Tennessee, Summitt grew up in Ashland City where, in 1985, Cheatham County High School named its gymnasium in her honor.

Before receiving the first of two degrees in physical education from the University of Tennessee, a bachelor of arts at Martin in 1974, and a master of arts in 1975 at Knoxville, Summitt was winning national team positions and international medals. The honors and the awards she garnered as a player continued even as she took on her first coaching job at the university, studied for a graduate degree, taught physical education and worked to repair a severely injured knee.

1973   World University Games in U.S.S.R.,
       Co-captain, Silver;

1975   Pan American Games in Mexico,
       Gold;

1976   XXI Olympic Games in Canada,
       Co-captain, Silver.

In 16 years, with three NCAA titles, [only three men in the NCAA have won more titles: John Wooden of the University of California-Los Angeles, Adolph Rupp of the University of Kentucky and Indiana University's Bobby Knight] Summitt has taken eleven teams into the NCAA Final Four, 14 of her players have been All-

American and eight have been on U.S. Olympic teams.

Summitt also has coached numerous U.S. championship teams:

1977   Jr. Women's National Basketball, California,
        Gold;

1977   Women's Pan American Confederation, Mexico,
        Gold;

1979   Women's Pan American Games, Puerto Rico,
        Silver;

1979   Women in the William R. Jones Cup Games, Taiwan
        Gold;

1979   Women's World Championship Basketball, Korea,
        Gold;

1980   Women's World Championship Basketball, Brazil,[2]
        Silver;

1983   Converse Coach of the Year
        WBCA* Coach of the Year;

1984   XXIII Olympic Games, California,
        Gold;

1987, 1989 and 1994
        Naismith Coach of the Year;

Summitt credits her family as the greatest influence in her life. She learned responsibility, discipline and hard work from her parents; and the competitive struggle for success came with three older brothers and a younger sister.

There were always chores to be done after school and basketball with her brothers was a fierce two-on-two drive. "I think that my brothers and I had to compete for everything. ... I don't know whether it was something I developed or I was born with it. But I've had a driving force inside me to compete and be successful in competition. ... I hate to lose to this day. I don't handle it well."

Successful competition has produced more awards of distinction for Summitt than can be listed. From "Who's Who of American Women" to Outstanding Young Women of America 1978 through 1981, and the Round Table Award of Christians and Jews, she is recognized as one of the nation's outstanding team leaders. In 1990, Summitt was inducted into the International Women's Sports Hall of Fame.

Summitt is praised by peers, players and fans. At just the mention of her name, a taxi driver in Knoxville and a business executive flying cross-country both gave this author unsolicited testimony to her skill and their excitement in watching her involvement with the players as the games unfold.

Home for Summitt is with husband R.B., and four-year-old son Tyler in Knoxville. When time permits, running, boating and skiing are favored activities.

Summitt, the author of a textbook titled "Basketball," was an early and enthusiastic supporter of this book; we are grateful she didn't tell us of the work ahead or the time it would consume.

Judith M. Sweet was appointed Director of Athletics and Supervisor of Physical Education at the University of California-San Diego, in 1975, after one year as assistant director. She was the first, and for many years the only, woman in the United States to head a joint athletic program for men and women at a major university. But "firsts" are a part of her record:

1989   NCAA Secretary Treasurer, a two-year term;

1991   NCAA President, a two-year term.

Sweet was elected in 1983 to the NCAA Council—a committee that establishes and directs general policy. After a two-year term, she was reelected to a four-year term. As a member of many NCAA committees during and since that time, and with full understanding of the opposition to female presence in the NCAA "man's world," she feels a strong commitment to the women and minorities who follow in her path.

Posted in her office, as a reminder of the struggle faced by women and minorities in sports-related careers, is a column from the *Atlanta Constitution* that said: "The installation of a woman as NCAA president befuddles me. ... Sweet is no doubt quite a competent person, but this is mainly a male organization, and I consider her ascension as pure tokenism."

Born January 19, 1948, in Milwaukee, Wisconsin, Sweet grew up with two older brothers and several male cousins, who included her in most of their activities. Considered a tomboy by some, she looks back on her early years and a preference for baseball and football with the boys, as a most valuable introduction to the male-dominated sports world.

At the University of Wisconsin-Madison, Sweet earned a bachelor of science degree with honors in physical education in 1969. Then came

117

her first job as a coach and instructor at Newcomb College-Tulane University, New Orleans.

In 1970 Sweet moved to the University of Arizona, Tucson, as a physical education instructor and badminton coach. At the same time she worked on a graduate degree in education, which she received in 1972, again with honors.

Before moving to the University of California in 1973, Sweet taught physical education at Kearny High School in San Diego. At the university, as assistant director of athletics and supervisor of physical education, she coached the varsity men's and women's badminton team to a conference championship.

In 1981, Sweet was graduated with distinction from the Master of Business Administration program at National University, San Diego.

Sweet's list of honors has been growing since 1969, when she achieved Mortar Board and Phi Kappa Phi honor society. Included in "Who's Who of American Women," Sweet also has been Woman and Administrator of the Year, given honorary lifetime membership and achievement awards or their equivalents by universities, national associations and magazines, newspapers, and government bodies.

Honorary doctorates were bestowed on her in 1993 by The United States Sports Academy, Daphne, Alabama and Monmouth College, West Long Branch, New Jersey. The honors continue.

Although she loves a challenge, Sweet is sometimes surprised at what she has accomplished. Often asked if her success and position fulfills a lifelong dream, she told *USA Today*: "... not in my wildest dreams could I have anticipated the opportunities that I've had. There weren't even athletic programs for girls or women at the time I was growing up. ... So, we've seen some dramatic changes."

Sweet gives high praise to the reform era that accompanied her NCAA presidency: "While we may not be able to solve all the problems at one time, I think we're identifying the appropriate priorities ... and demonstrating that we have the courage to make changes." For Sweet, "The focal point is academic standards. This will result in a better prepared student with greater potential to graduate and meet responsibilities all through life."

Sweet's career takes up most of her time. But at home in La Jolla, she has served her community as president of the Homeowners Association for 13 years. In addition to being an officer and committee member in local, state and national organizations, she is a lecturer and author of a chapter in a book for athletic programs, "Organizational Management Administration," by Tom Kinder.

Tara VanDerveer, born June 26, 1953, in Melrose, Massachusetts, is self-described as "driven," "focused" and "absolutely intrigued by the game of basketball." And the "intrigue" started at an early age. She laughs when relating the story of a librarian's concerned call to her father: "Tara has read every basketball book in the library, and they are all about boys."

But, the fascination and the voracious reading produced results. "When it comes to awards, one of the things I was most proud of is the fact that the ninth grade boy's gym teacher wrote in my yearbook, 'To the best basketball player, boy or girl, in the ninth grade.' That was really

121

important to me," she said, "because I didn't even play on a team."

VanDerveer continues to study what separates successful people from everyone else; "...what makes them really good at things and how they work, then I model after them." she said. This study habit also prompted her daily presence for three years at Indiana University men's basketball team practice. In the same three years, she was a starting guard for the women's basketball team and a dean's list student. VanDerveer received a bachelor of arts in sociology in 1975.

After earning a master of arts in sport management from Ohio State University in Columbus, VanDerveer headed women's basketball at the University of Idaho, Moscow, for two years. She brought unprecedented success to the team with a 1980 conference championship and participation in the AIAW [The governing body for women before the NCAA.] playoffs.

In 1980, it was back to Ohio State to coach women's basketball for five years, build championship teams and an award-winning record:

1982, 1984 and 1985
  Big Ten Champions;

1983 Big Ten Co-Champions;

1984 and 1985
  Big Ten Coach of the Year.

In 1985, VanDerveer was appointed head coach of Stanford University women's basketball program. Although she acknowledges a natural shyness and discomfort in the center of attention, her leadership skills and her success with the Stanford Cardinal teams have placed her on national television, in "Who's Who of American Women," and made her a prominent national sports figure.

1988 WBNS* National Coach of the Year
  WBCA District VIII Coach of the Year

1989 PAC-10* first team with a perfect conference season
  Converse National Coach of the Year
  WBCA District VIII Coach of the Year
  PAC-10 Coach of the Year

1990 NCAA Championship
  PAC-10 Co-Championship
  Naismith Coach of the Year
  WBCA District VIII Coach of the Year
  PAC-10 Coach of the Year

1991 NCAA Final Four
  PAC-10 Championship;

1992   NCAA Championship;

1993   PAC-10 Championship, fifth consecutive year.

VanDerveer also coaches on the international court:

1986   East team at the U.S. Olympic Festival, Houston, Texas;

1990   U.S. "B" team in Yugoslavia and the U.S.S.R.;

1991   U.S. World University Games, Sheffield, England, Gold;

1993   World Championship Qualifying Tournament, Sao Paulo, Brazil, Gold;

1994   FIBA World Championship, Sydney, Australia, Bronze;

1994   Goodwill Games, St. Petersburgh, Russia, Gold.

Happiest when building and maintaining team moral, VanDerveer credits much of her ability to a lifetime of strong family support. "I got a lot of love and attention from my parents, grandparents, my aunts and uncles. I feel like I have a battery that has a lot of voltage in it, and I am capable of giving a lot to other people."

The oldest of five children [she has three sisters and one brother] VanDerveer takes the game

124

and its players as personally as she does her family and friends. The important things in her life are personal events such as letters from and activities with the many people who touch her daily life.

VanDerveer has been running her own summer basketball camp at Stanford since 1985. The camp is a possible part of a future that may not include coaching a team. "I don't take myself real seriously," she said. "There are other things I want to do someday." That includes a desire to write children's books that would help to fill the void she discovered as a youngster in the library: "... success stories, women and children need that," she said.

John Robert Wooden is a sports legend. He is listed among the world's greatest leaders and still affectionately called "The Wizard of Westwood," in reference to and in honor of his 27 years of record-building achievement at the University of California, Los Angeles, as head basketball coach.

Selected as college Coach of the Year six times beginning in 1964, Wooden also set a number of other records in NCAA basketball history:

- 664-162 collegiate game wins-loses;

- 88 consecutive victories;

- 38 consecutive NCAA tournament victories;

- 16 PAC-8* championships;

- 10 NCAA championships;

- 8 undefeated PAC-8 championships;

- 7 consecutive NCAA championships;

- 4 undefeated full seasons.

Born October 14, 1910, in Martinsville, Indiana, Wooden has received honors from close-to-home friends and institutions, from national magazines and organizations, to international recognition that he considers his highest honor. In 1985 he became the first sports figure to be awarded the Bellarmine Medal of Excellence by Bellarmine College, Louisville, Kentucky, thereby joining such luminaries as Mother Teresa and Walter Cronkite.

Wooden cites his greatest accomplishment as the Big Ten Medal for Proficiency in Scholarship and Athletics, which he received in 1932 when he graduated from Purdue University, with a bachelor of arts in English.

He also remembers 1969 as a year for accepting honors of which he is particularly proud:

named Outstanding Basketball Coach of the United States by AP,* UPI* and NABC; nominated King and Grand Marshall of the Morgan County Fall Foliage Festival and Parade, and at the same time having a hometown street named for him. These multifaceted achievements are expressive of a man who believes that love and balance are the two most important words in life.

For three years in high school and in college, Wooden was an All State and All American basketball player, respectively. He led his high school team to a state title in 1927, and as runners-up in 1926 and 1928. In 1931 and 1932, with Wooden as captain, Purdue's Boilermakers won Big Ten titles and the 1932 National Collegiate championship; he was named college Player of the Year in 1932.

The next two years were spent at Dayton High School in Kentucky where he coached everything offered, and then came nine years teaching English, baseball, basketball and tennis at South Bend Central High School in Indiana.

Wooden served as a lieutenant in the U.S. Navy from 1943 to 1946, and then resumed his career as athletic director at Indiana State University in Terre Haute, for two years before his move to University of California-Los Angeles.

In 1943 Wooden also was selected by the Hall of Fame as a member of the All-Time All-American Basketball team; he was inducted into the National Basketball Hall of Fame as a player in 1960, and as a coach in 1972, making him the only two-category member.

During his years of coaching and now in his years of retirement, Wooden has received many honors for service to amateur athletics and American youth. Among those numerous awards are:

- Whitney Young Urban League Award for humanitarian service;

- "Coach of the Century" by the Friars Club;

- "Sports Man of the Year" by *Sporting News;*

- "Sportsman of the Year" by *Sports Illustrated;*

- Indiana Basketball Hall of Fame;

- "Velvet Covered Brick" award for Christian leadership.

The life and philosophy of the man with all these accolades was shaped by his father, whom he

respected as, "the smartest man I ever knew."
He remembers well that he and his three brothers were taught, "never try to be better than
someone else, always learn from others and
try to be the best you can be." Wooden's concern for character rather than reputation and
his ability to share his beliefs with others have
taken him from player and star athlete to coach
and one of this country's most admired leaders.

In August 1932, Wooden married his high
school sweetheart, Nellie Riley. Two children,
seven grandchildren and eight great grandchildren helped to make him "California Father of
the Year" in 1964 and "Grandfather of the
Year" in 1974.

As a published author of two books: "Practical
Modern Basketball" and "They Call Me
Coach," Wooden continues to write and lec-
ture as well as enjoy a heavy reading habit and
time with his family.

About the Authors

Close to 20 years of teamwork leadership experience has positioned Wendy Woodin Peche in the vanguard of problem solving on leadership and teamwork issues. She is the founder and leader of Teamwork by Design, a consulting and training business; an organizational development specialist for Wisconsin's largest employer in the vital health care industry; a member of the national speakers association; a graduate of the University of Wisconsin-Milwaukee Master's Degree Program in Administrative Leadership; and a former assistant professor on the same campus.

Peche was born and raised and is now working and living in and near Milwaukee. She and her husband, Leroy, have a young daughter. Peche relaxes in a canoe, on skis or on the golf course where she strives to maintain scratch golfer status.

About the Authors

Pat Gray Thomas is a writer, a former associate editor for *Advertising Age*, and a firm believer in teamwork with **LEGENDARY** leadership.

Thomas lives in Chicago with husband, Irving, whose publishing expertise has been thoroughly exploited in the writing of this book. She has four children and six grandchildren who come and go at various times of the year. Relaxation is with books, cross-country skis, walking the lakefront and sometimes bogey golf.

Index

Acronyms

AIAW   Association for Intercollegiate Athletics for Women
AP   The Associated Press
FIBA   International Federation for Basketball
NABC   National Association of Basketball Coaches
NAIA   National Association of Intercollegiate Athletics
NBA   National Basketball Association
NCAA   National Collegiate Athletics Association
PAC-8   Pacific-8
PAC-10 Pacific-10
UCLA   University of California-Los Angeles
UPI   United Press International
WBCA   Women's Basketball Coaches Association
WBNS   Women's Basketball News Service
WSUC   Wisconsin State University Conference

Footnotes

1   Gibran, K. The Prophet. New York, New York; Alfred A. Knopf Publisher, 1969

2   Summitt served as assistant coach to Sue Gunter of Lousiana State University-Baton Rouge.